WHAT IS THE 4TH OF JULY?

Elaine Landau

Enslow Elementary
an imprint of
Enslow Publishers, Inc.
40 Industrial Road
Box 398
Berkeley Heights, NJ 07922
USA

http://www.enslow.com

CONTENTS

WORDS TO KNOW 3

A SPECIAL TIME 5

HAPPY BIRTHDAY USA 6

A FIGHT FOR FREEDOM 9

RED, WHITE, AND BLUE 10

GREAT FOOD 12

OUTDOOR FUN 14

FIREWORKS 17

PROUD TO BE AN AMERICAN 18

AN ALL-AMERICAN CRAFT GAME 20

LEARN MORE: BOOKS 22

WEB SITES 23

INDEX 24

WORDS TO KNOW

celebrate (SEL uh brayt)—
To have a good time or enjoy
yourself.

independence (in dee PEN dens)—
To be free and able to make your
own choices.

nation (NAY shun)—A large area of
land with many people. It is usually
free to make its own rules.

A SPECIAL TIME

What a great day! Soldiers, bands, and scouts march in parades. People wave flags and cheer. Fireworks light the sky. It must be the 4th of July!

HAPPY BIRTHDAY
USA

You have a birthday. The United States has one, too. Our nation was born on July 4, 1776. Before that, England ruled the land. But the Americans did not like being ruled by a king.

A FIGHT FOR
FREEDOM

Americans said they wanted their
independence on July 4, 1776.
They had to fight England. They
wanted to be free. It was not easy.
America and England had a war.
After five years, America won.

RED, WHITE, AND BLUE

The 4th of July is also called Independence Day.

Now the United States is a free country. It celebrates the 4th of July every year. People fly flags. They wear red, white, and blue. Those are the colors of our flag.

GREAT FOOD

There are lots of picnics. Some people cook and eat at a park. The hot dogs are tasty. People eat corn on the cob. They eat watermelon, too. Enjoy some red, white, and blue desserts!

OUTDOOR
FUN

Some people go swimming in lakes and pools.
Others hike or run races. Still others play ball.
There are outdoor concerts, too. Bands play songs.
People sing along.

FIREWORKS

At night there are fireworks. They light up the dark sky. Boom, boom! We think of the soldiers who fought and died for our freedom.

PROUD TO BE AN
AMERICAN

The 4th of July is a time to be proud.
Americans are lucky. We live in the
land of the free and the home of the
brave. We celebrate this every 4th
of July.

AN
ALL-AMERICAN CRAFT GAME

Have some fun with your friends on the 4th of July!

You Will Need:

❖ 10 white index cards

❖ 10 wooden craft sticks

❖ tape

❖ red marker

❖ blue marker

❖ silver stick-on stars

What to Do:

1. Draw and color in a blue square in the upper left corner of the index cards.

2. Stick some silver stars on the blue squares.

3. Draw red stripes on the cards.

4. Tape a craft stick to the back of each index card.

5. Write these words on the back of each card: "I love America because . . ."

6. Give each of your friends a flag. Let each person finish the sentence. Why do you love America?

LEARN MORE

BOOKS

Aloian, Molly. *Independence Day*. New York: Crabtree, 2010.

Court, Rob. *How to Draw Independence Day Things*. Mankato, Minn.: Child's World, 2006.

Heinrichs, Ann. *Independence Day*. Chanhassen, Minn.: Child's World, 2006.

Mercer, Abbie. *Happy 4th of July*. New York: PowerKids Press, 2008.

Trueit, Trudi Strain. *Independence Day*. New York: Children's Press, 2007.

WEB SITES

Celebrate Independence Day
http://www.kidsturncentral.com/holidays/july4.htm

USA Coloring Pages
http://www.dltk-kids.com/usa/musaposter.html

INDEX

A
America, 9
Americans, 6, 9, 18
B
bands, 5, 14
birthday, 6
C
celebrate, 8, 10, 18
concerts, 14
E
England, 6, 9

F
fireworks, 5, 17
flags, 10
food, 12
freedom, 9, 10, 17, 18
I
independence, 9
J
July 4, 1776, 6, 9

N
nation, 6
O
outdoor activities, 14
P
parades, 5
picnics, 12
R
red, white, and blue, 10

S
scouts, 5
soldiers, 5, 17
songs, 14
U
United States, 6, 10
W
war, 9

Enslow Elementary, an imprint of Enslow Publishers, Inc.
Enslow Elementary® is a registered trademark of Enslow Publishers, Inc.

Copyright © 2012 by Elaine Landau

Library of Congress Cataloging-in-Publication Data
Landau, Elaine.
  What is the 4th of July? / by Elaine Landau.
    p. cm. — (I like holidays!)
  Includes index.
  Summary: "An introduction to the 4th of July with an easy activity"— Provided by publisher.
  ISBN 978-0-7660-3703-8
  1. Fourth of July—Juvenile literature. I. Title.
  E286.A1388 2010
  394.2634—dc22
                                    2010039478

Paperback ISBN 978-1-59845-292-1

Printed in China
052011 Leo Paper Group, Heshan City, Guangdong, China
10 9 8 7 6 5 4 3 2 1

To Our Readers: We have done our best to make sure all Internet Addresses in this book were active and appropriate when we went to press. However, the author and the publisher have no control over and assume no liability for the material available on those Internet sites or on other Web sites they may link to. Any comments or suggestions can be sent by e-mail to comments@enslow.com or to the address on the back cover.

Photo Credits: Associated Press, pp. 4, 5, 15; iStockphoto.com: © Eileen Hart, p. 23, © Steve Debenport, p. 13; © Photos.com, p. 1; Shutterstock.com, pp. 2, 3, 7, 10, 11, 12, 16, 19, 20; Tamika Moore/Birmingham News/Landov, p. 14; U.S. Center of Military History, p. 8.

Cover Photo: © Photos.com

Series Consultant:
Duncan R. Jamieson, PhD
Professor of History
Ashland University
Ashland, OH

Series Literacy Consultant:
Allan A. De Fina, PhD
Dean, College of Education/Professor of Literacy Education
New Jersey City University
Past President of the New Jersey Reading Association